Current Hits

for Students

8 Graded Selections for Intermediate Pianists

Arranged by

Carol Matz

Students of all ages love playing popular pieces by their favorite recording artists. This collection includes accessible arrangements of pop hits by Katy Perry, Cee Lo Green, Paramore, Travie McCoy, Plain White T's, Christina Perri and Michael Bublé. The arrangements are "teacher friendly," while remaining faithful to the sound of the original recording. In this intermediate collection, 16th-note rhythms are introduced, as well as octaves and increased left-hand arpeggiation.

Alfred

Produced by
Alfred Music Publishing Co., Inc.
P.O. Box 10003
Van Nuys, CA 91410-0003
alfred.com

Printed in USA.

ISBN-10: 0-7390-8631-6
ISBN-13: 978-0-7390-8631-5

FORGET YOU

Words and Music by Christopher Brown, Peter Hernandez,
Ari Levine, Philip Lawrence and Thomas "Cee Lo" Callaway
Arranged by Carol Matz

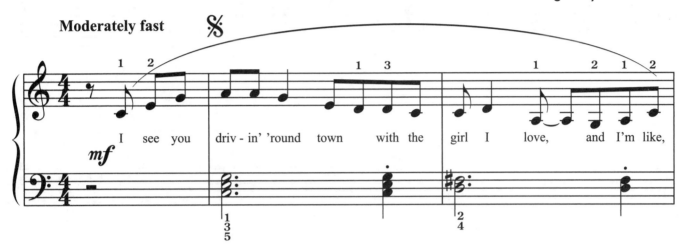

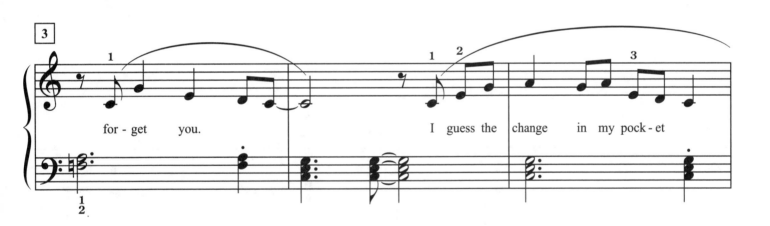

4

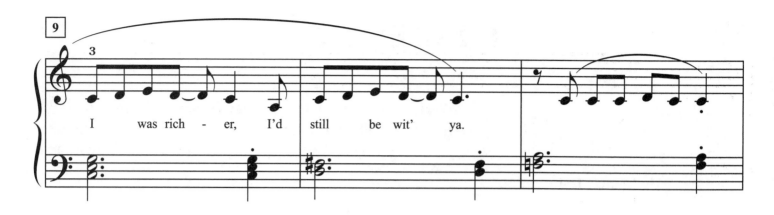

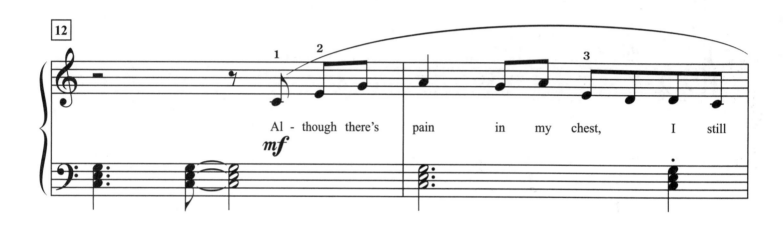

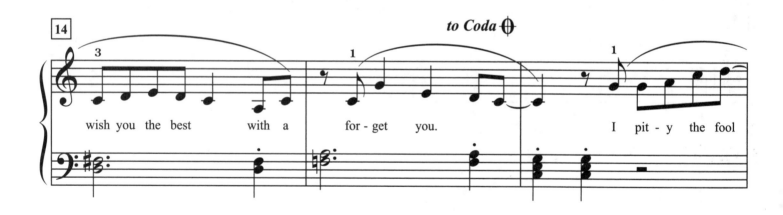

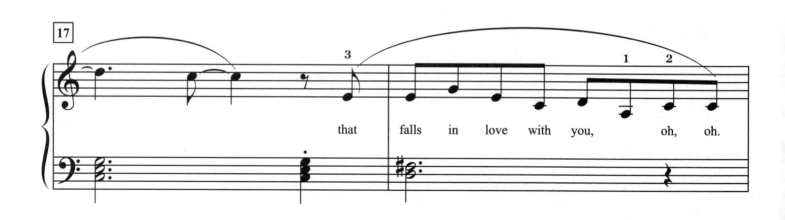

(Oh, she's a gold - dig - ger. Just thought you should know it.)

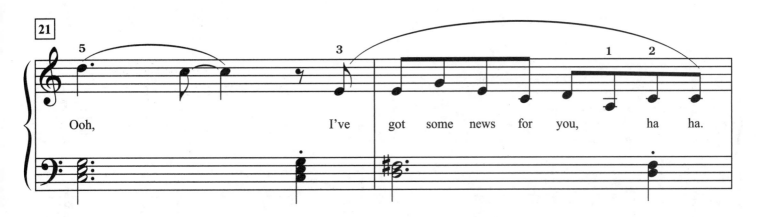

Ooh, I've got some news for you, ha ha.

D.S. al Coda

See you

Coda

BILLIONAIRE

Words and Music by Peter Hernandez,
Ari Levine, Philip Lawrence and Travis McCoy
Arranged by Carol Matz

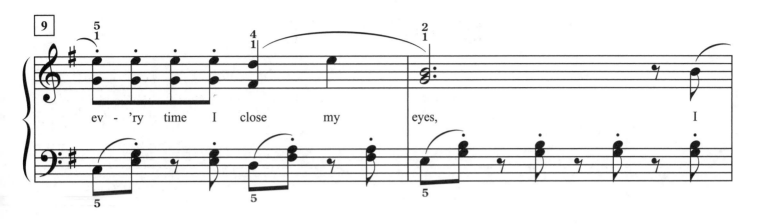

ev - 'ry time I close my eyes, I

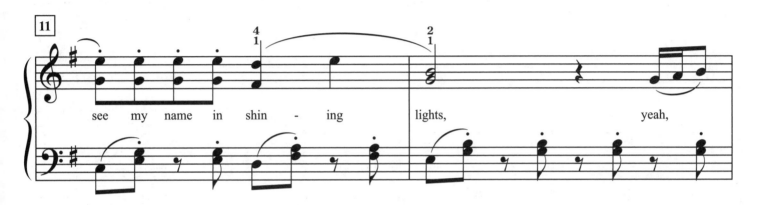

see my name in shin - ing lights, yeah,

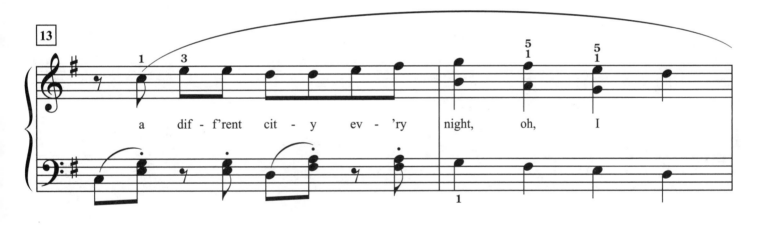

a dif - f'rent cit - y ev - 'ry night, oh, I

swear, the world bet - ter pre - pare for when I'm a bil - lion -

aire. Oh, oh, when I'm a bil - lion -

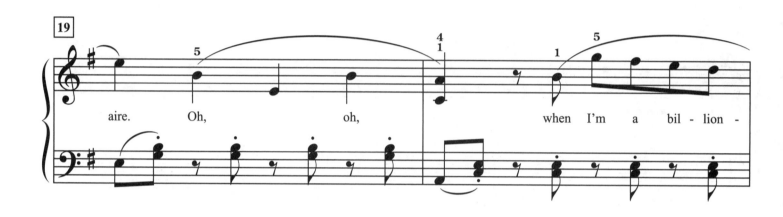

aire. Oh, oh, when I'm a bil - lion -

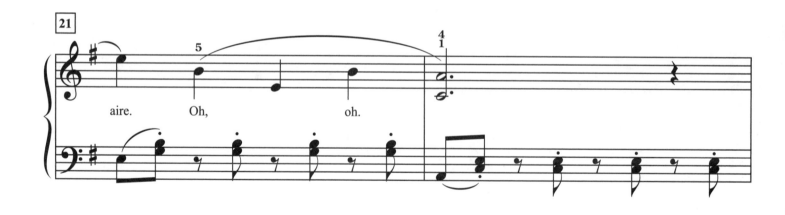

aire. Oh, oh.

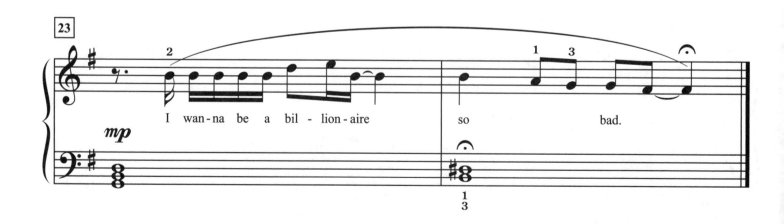

I wan-na be a bil - lion-aire so bad.

NOT LIKE THE MOVIES

Words and Music by Katy Perry and Greg Wells
Arranged by Carol Matz

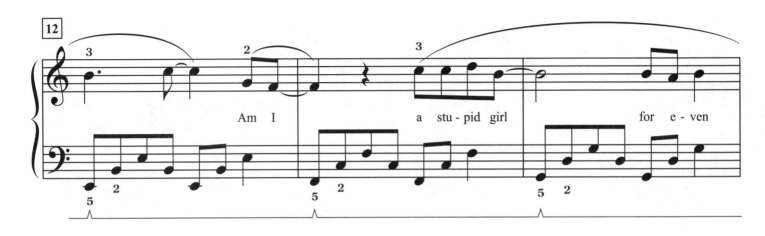

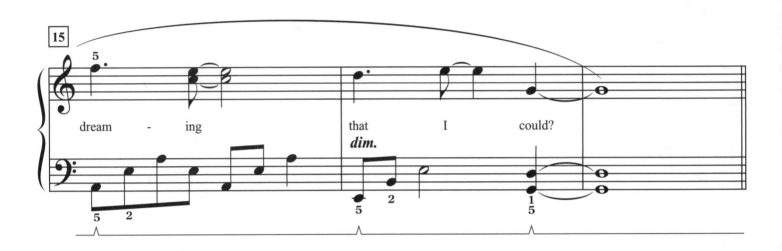

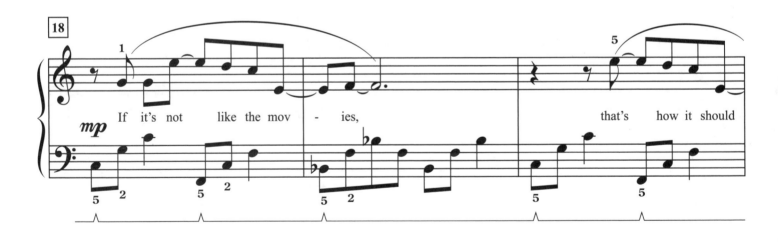

spin - ning.　　　　　And that's just　　the be - gin - ning.

It's not　　like the mov　- ies,　　　　but that's　　how it should

be.　　yeah.　　　　When he's the one, you'll come un - done,　and your world　will stop

spin - ning.　　　　　And it's just　　the be - gin - ning.

FIREWORK

Words and Music by Katy Perry, Mikkel Eriksen,
Tor Erik Hermansen, Sandy Wilhelm and Ester Dean
Arranged by Carol Matz

13

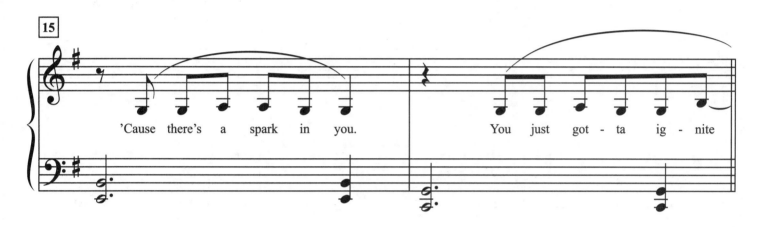

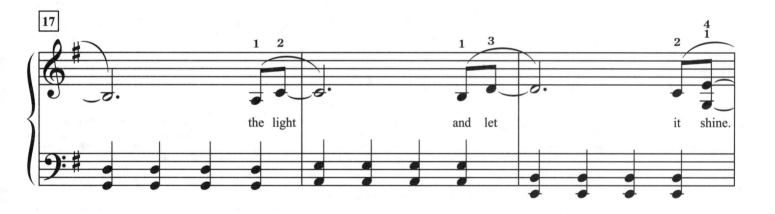

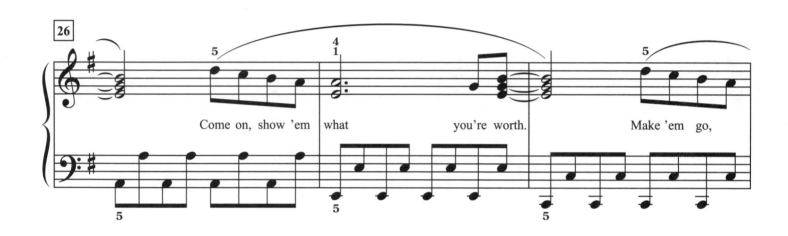

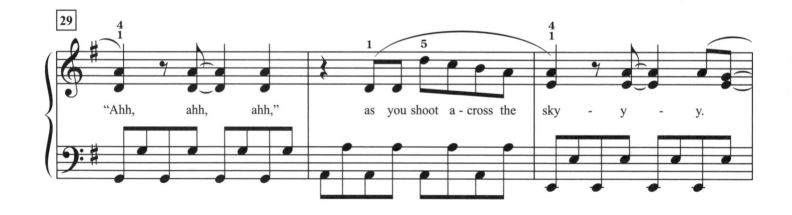

col - ors burst.   Make 'em go,   "Ahh,   ahh,   ahh."

You're gon - na leave them all in awe,   awe,   awe.

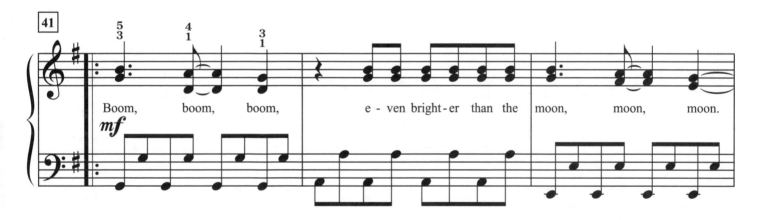

Boom,   boom,   boom,   e - ven bright-er than the moon,   moon,   moon.

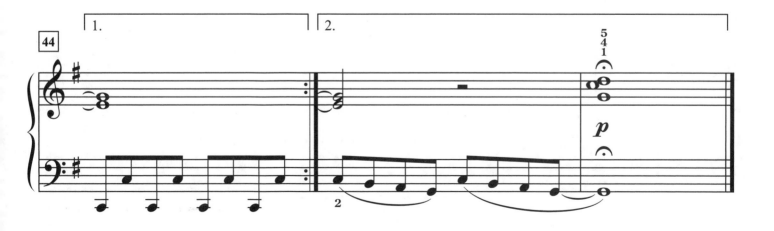

1.

2.

HEY THERE DELILAH

Words and Music by Tom Higgenson
Arranged by Carol Matz

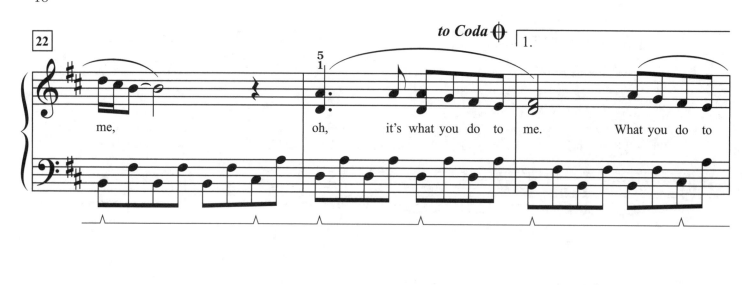

to Coda ⊕

me, oh, it's what you do to me. What you do to

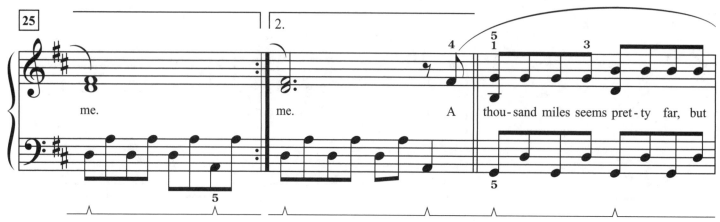

me. me. A thou-sand miles seems pret-ty far, but

they've got planes and trains and cars. I'd walk to you if I had no oth-er

way. Our friends would all make fun of us, and we'll just laugh a-long be-cause we

know that none of them have felt this way. De - li - lah, I can pro-mise you that

by the time that we get through, the world will nev - er, ev - er be the

D.S. al Coda

same, and you're to blame.

Coda

me. What you do to me.

JAR OF HEARTS

Words and Music by Drew Lawrence,
Christina Perri and Barrett Yeretsian
Arranged by Carol Matz

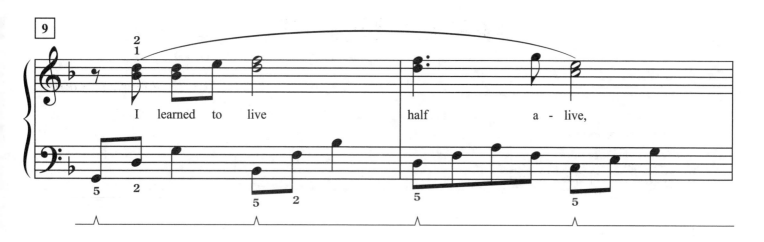

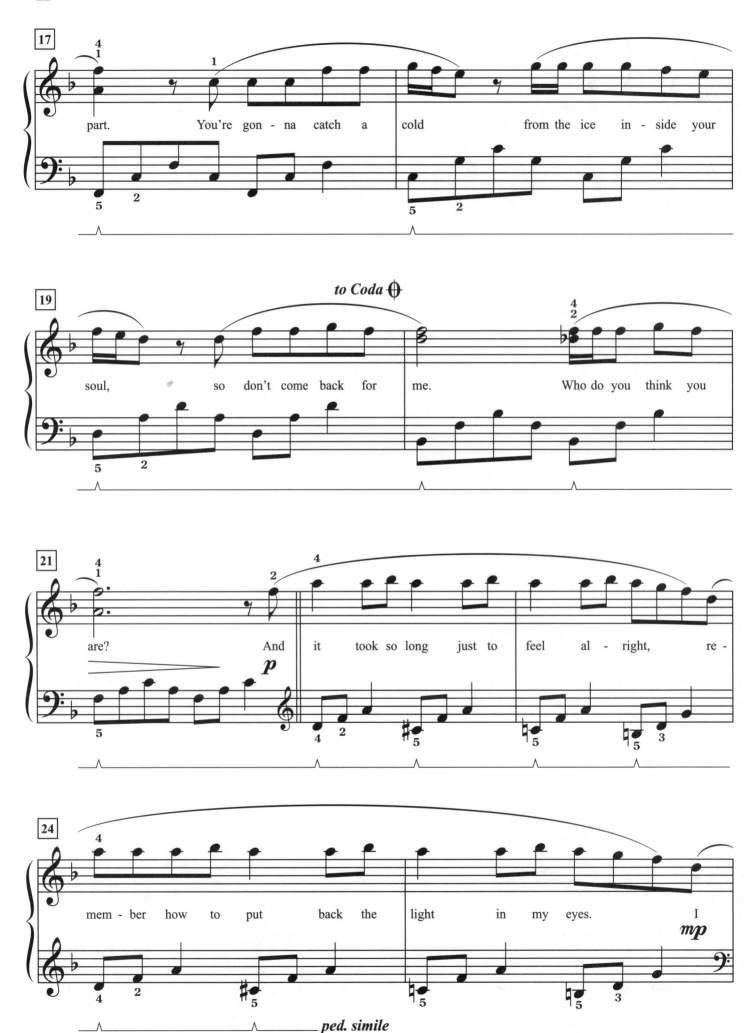

THE ONLY EXCEPTION

Words and Music by Hayley Williams and Josh Farro
Arranged by Carol Matz

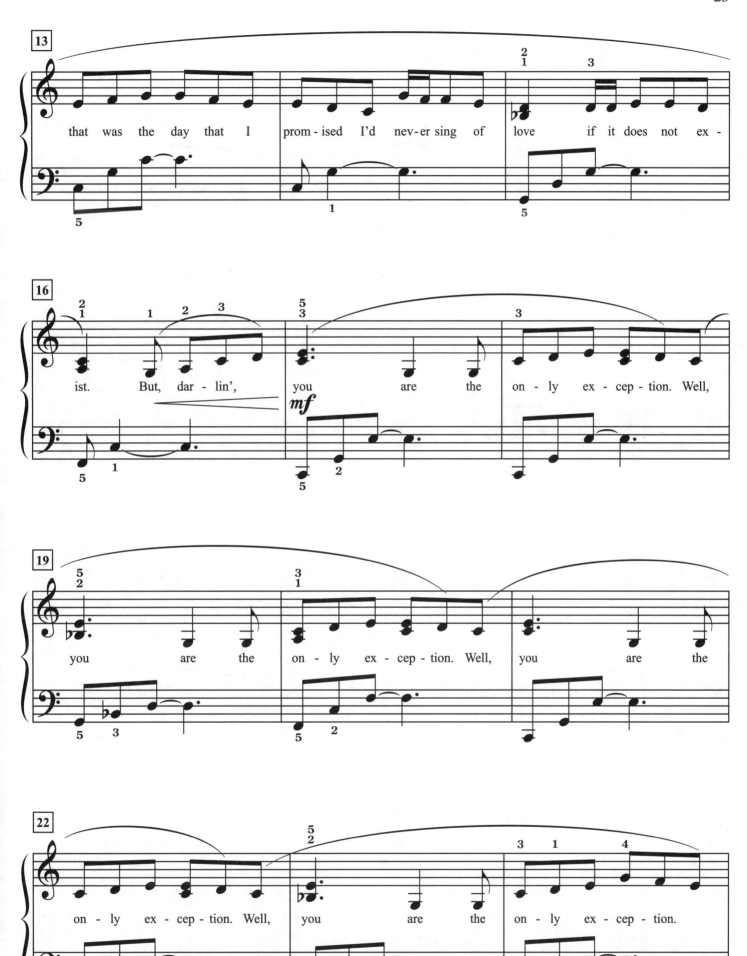

leav - ing   in the morn - ing when you   wake   up.   Leave me   with some kind of proof it's   not a

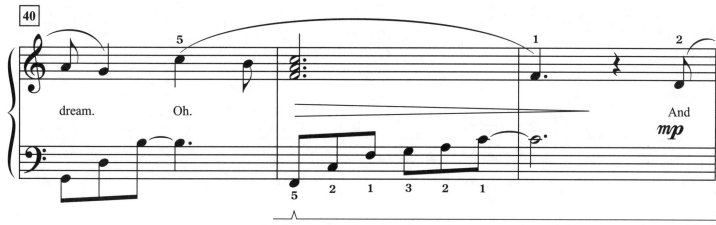

dream.   Oh.

And

I'm   on   my   way   to   be - liev - ing.

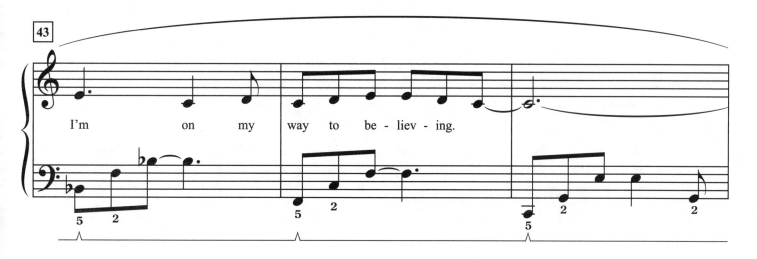

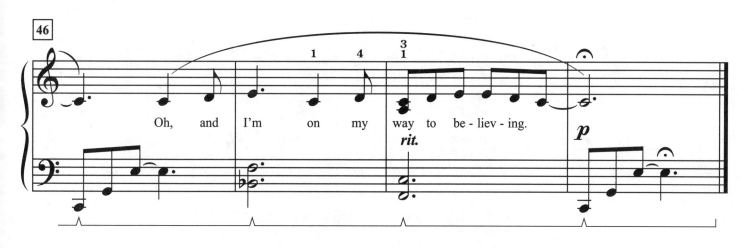

Oh,   and   I'm   on   my   way   to   be - liev - ing.

look + listen!

EVERYTHING

Words and Music by Michael Bublé,
Alan Chang and Amy Foster
Arranged by Carol Matz

30

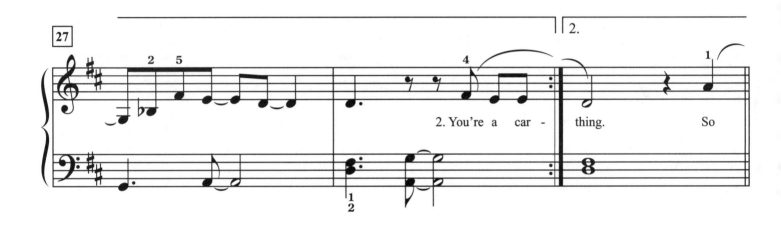

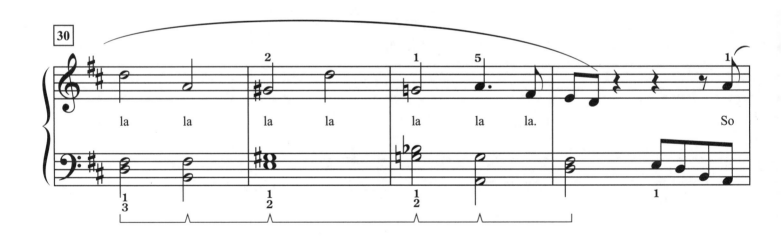

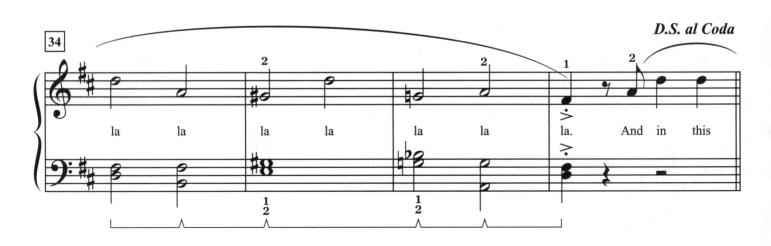